Happy Talk

Also by Jesse Eisenberg

Bream Gives Me Hiccups

The Spoils: A Play

The Revisionist: A Play

Asuncion: A Play

Happy Talk

A Play

JESSE EISENBERG

Grove Press
New York

FIRST EDITION

Published simultaneously in Canada
Printed in the United States of America

First Grove Atlantic paperback edition: December 2019

This book is set in 11-point Bembo by Alpha Design & Composition of Pittsfield, NH

Library of Congress Cataloging-in-Publication data is available for this title.

ISBN 978-0-8021-4801-8
eISBN 978-0-8021-4802-5

Grove Press
an imprint of Grove Atlantic
154 West 14th Street
New York, NY 10011

Distributed by Publishers Group West

groveatlantic.com

19 20 21 22   10 9 8 7 6 5 4 3 2 1

Happy Talk

.

PRODUCTION CREDITS

Happy Talk was originally produced by The New Group (Scott El-liott, Artistic Director; Adam Bernstein, Executive Director), opening on April 30, 2019, at The Pershing Square Signature Center in New York City. It was directed by Scott Elliott; Set Design: Derek McLane; Costume Design: Clint Ramos; Lighting Design: Jeff Croiter; Sound Design: Rob Milburn and Michael Bodeen; Fight Direction: Unkle-Dave's Fight-House; Production Supervisor: Five Ohm Productions; Production Stage Manager: Valerie A. Peterson.

The cast was as follows:

Lorraine	Susan Sarandon
Ljuba	Marin Ireland
Bill	Daniel Oreskes
Ronny	Nico Santos
Jenny	Tedra Millan

A suburban kitchen and living room. It's 1990s, unrenovated, with sliding glass doors that lead out to the porch and backyard. There is a staircase that leads offstage, with an exposed landing area.

It is nighttime.

BILL is 65 years old, nursing a scotch and reading a thick book about the Civil War.

LJUBA, a forty-year-old Serbian woman with bleached blonde hair, smokes a cigarette outside. She speaks on her cell phone, in Serbian. She's agitated and occasionally yelling.

An irritating electronic beep sounds, coming from offstage. Ljuba does not hear it.

Bill looks up, apathetically, and then retreats back into his book.

After a minute, the beep sounds again.

Finally, a series of insistent beeps. Ljuba leans her head against the glass door and hears the beeps. She stubs out her cigarette and enters the house.

Ljuba begins to change her shirt into a shirt she has crumpled and left by the door. She removes her shoes for indoor slippers.

LJUBA   I'm sorry Mr. Bill, was she calling a long time?

Bill shrugs.

I can't stop smoking today, I'm sorry. I'm not in a good way today, I'm sorry, Mr. Bill.

1

Bill shakes his head, indicating that it's okay.

I know it smells disgusting to you. It smells disgusting to me too. And also the taste. (*calls toward the offstage bedroom*) I'm coming Ruthie. I was just in the bathroom. I'm coming!

At the sink, Ljuba washes the cigarette smell out of her mouth.

The whole thing is disgusting. Did I tell you what she tells me one time? She tells me that she don't like it if I smoke cigarette because it means I am a stupid person and she don't want to be with stupid people. She actually tell me, "I *like* the smell of *cigarette*, but I *don't* like the smell of *stupid*." So is interesting, in some way.

Bill looks up and acknowledges her.

Excuse me.

Ljuba exits into the bedroom—

(*os*) Ah, you just pee. Is no problem, Ruthie. (*calls to Bill*) She just pee, is no problem, Mr. Bill!

Ljuba reenters, grabs a box of Fig Newtons from the pantry and begins plating a few.

She pee again. I don't know why. I change her diaper five minutes ago and she pee again. The coffee—is like it wants to *race* through her body today. I give her the coffee, I wait five minutes and poof! She pee. And I know is the coffee because the pee *smell* like coffee. It actually smell *just* like coffee. Is hazelnut, so is easy to know. Next time, I maybe just pour the coffee right onto the diaper, is faster.

Bill places his scotch down on the table.

What?

Bill nods toward the drink.

She is going to want her cookie.

He stares at her.

2

Okay, I take a little sip.

Ljuba takes a little sip. She calms.

Thank you.

Bill nods, sweetly.

Now I'm definitely going to want a cigarette.

It's calm for a moment before we hear a beep.

Her cookie—

Ljuba disappears back into the room with the Fig Newtons.

Bill takes his drink and sips. The house is quiet.

LORRAINE, nearing 60, enters. She is a whirlwind, flying around the room as she prepares Bill's dinner from premade food in Tupperware.

LORRAINE Hello there, Lootellan! I'm sorry I'm late, we went over a little bit. Which was all my fault! I was improvising during my introduction scene in Act One, which everybody just loves! I don't even know how I do it. It's like I leave my body and enter some kind of fantasy! Like I'm floating above the stage!

And when I come back down, I don't even know what I've said. But of course, everyone tells me. *You had this great bit about peanuts,* or *I was dying when you mentioned the orphans! Just dying!*

Those are just examples, it could be anything! Of course, it helps to be surrounded by such a wonderful ensemble. Everyone—well, *mostly* everyone—is so supportive. They're what make *me* possible. "You're only as good as those around you." Who said that? Eleanor Roosevelt? Was it Eleanor? Someone like her. She was such a great role model—such a *strong* woman, which I love.

She pecks Bill on the top of his head.

Anyway, you must be absolutely famished, sweetheart. I am so sorry I kept you waiting.

She begins plating the food.

3

And we open in three weeks, which is so exciting. Initially, I was a little skeptical of doing *South Pacific* at the Jewish Community Center. I thought it would be impossible to really *transport* the audience to Polynesia but James Peter does *wonders* with flats and I think it's all really coming together!

And Bloody Mary is just the most dynamic character in the show. I mean, we're laughing at her—she's funny, in her way, *loping* around the stage surrounded by these strapping GIs—but, really, she's a broken woman. (*a sincere beat as she considers her role*) She's a severely broken women. (*and then immediately upbeat*) So—what are you reading?

Bill doesn't respond.

Oh really. That sounds fascinating, honey. I'm glad we're sharing our interests and curiosities with each other. I, for example, just started a wonderful novel about a young woman who witnesses a murder in Italy, which I absolutely love because you have the *mystery* element because of the murder and the *exotic* element because of it being in Italy.

And you, Bill, are reading—drumroll please—

She makes a big show of going over to him and ducking down to see the title of his book.

—*The Civil War: America in Crisis*. Oh god, Bill, another book about the Civil War? Honey, that is such an old man thing to do. Right before every man dies, they read a book about the Civil War. It's like a right of passage for the River Styx. You must pay the fee and also tell me what happened at Appomattox. Is that what you want, Bill? To die? Because that's where you're headed. It is a one-way street.

She sets up a personal tray stand in front of Bill and places the plate of food atop. Bill begins eating with his hands, even though there is a fork and knife.

Here's your food, sweetie, be careful, it's hot. God. I really am surrounded by dying people.

Lorraine now fixes herself a plate.

4

You want me to be all alone here? Bill? Can you picture that? If you die? I'l be all alone. I wouldn't know what to do with myself, if you die. I wouldn't know what to do with all this space.

BILL   I'm sure you'll figure something out.

Lorraine is rattled by his sudden interjection—

You're very crafty.

LORRAINE   Ljuba! Ljuba!

LJUBA (*os*)   I'm coming!

Ljuba enters with a sippy cup and a box of Fig Newtons. Lorraine is relieved.

LORRAINE   Hello sweetheart—how are you today?

LJUBA   Honestly, I am not that good. Unfortunately, I—

LORRAINE (*doesn't acknowledge*)   Well, give me a peck.

Ljuba kisses Lorraine on both cheeks.

Just like the French! I love it!

LJUBA   You a little late, no?

LORRAINE   Just a tad, sweetheart, I got caught up in character— during my introduction scene, you know—and they practically had to *lobotomize* me to bring me back.

LJUBA   How was your practice?

LORRAINE   My *rehearsal*? It was divine. I'm doing what I love. What could be better? I'm one of the lucky ones. So how's the beast? Did she take her her meds?

LJUBA   She spit the trazodone out right into my hand. She tell me it make her mouth taste like nickels.

LORRAINE   Nickels?

LJUBA Yes, she say it taste like nickels in her mouth in the morning. I ask her: Would you be more happy if it taste like quarters? You know, because is more money.

LORRAINE That's cute.

LJUBA Thank you. So I joke with her but she don't want to laugh—

LORRAINE (*wry*) That's too bad, we used to have so much fun together. Hide it in her applesauce.

LJUBA I already did.

LORRAINE That's why I love you. Listen: the important thing is that we keep her alive so that she can continue contributing to society so magnanimously.

LJUBA Lorraine, is not funny—

LORRAINE Oh, come on, it's a little funny.

Lorraine opens the door and calls in to her mother:

Yes, thank you Mom, for your beneficence and grace! May your dirty diapers nourish the hungry and your drool quench the thirsty.

LJUBA I am not laughing.

LORRAINE And should you ever figure out what day it is, may your brain be harvested for science!

LJUBA Lorraine!

LORRAINE I know, I'm horrible. I'm sorry—

LJUBA Don't you be sorry. Is normal. I was speaking with my daughter earlier, she says a terrible thing to me—

LORRAINE That's different.

LJUBA How is different?

LORRAINE   Because my mother spent her life torturing me. You've sacrificed everything for that ungrateful young woman. Sending your daughter all your money every month so she can sleep 'til noon—

LJUBA   She can't find a job—

LORRAINE   And date that horrid man—Dragon?

LJUBA   *Dragan*, you close. They buy a dog yesterday.

LORRAINE   A dog? Who does she think she is, the Queen of England?

LJUBA   I know, exactly! I tell her today over the phone: "You cannot take care of your own self, how are you going to take care of a dog, too?" You know what she say?

LORRAINE   Something in Serbian?

LJUBA   She hang up on me.

LORRAINE   At least she calls you. My daughter hasn't called me in months, she hates me. She's probably joined a cult, which would at least provide her with some discipline.

LJUBA   She probably does not hate you.

LORRAINE   You haven't met her.

LJUBA   If I would meet your daughter, I would say: "respect your mother."

LORRAINE   Well, thank you. That's not very deep or original, but I appreciate you standing up for me in the hypothetical. And if I ever wind up in Serbia—which, I'm sorry, is at the very bottom of my places to visit—I'm gonna track down your little Raggedy Ann and slap that girl in the face—

LJUBA   Lorraine! Is my daughter!

LORRAINE   My god, I'm so sorry sweetheart. I would never hit another person. I'm sorry—I'm just angry at my own daughter and *projecting* onto your daughter. When you speak to her next, apologize for me. She's probably a lovely young woman. I'd like to meet her one day. If it's convenient.

Lorraine has finished making her plate and is sitting at the table.

Did you want to eat something too?

LJUBA No, I'm fine. I will eat when you are done. When Bill go upstairs, I eat. I don't want to be in the way. You *staring* at a person eating, the food going in and out, is not comfortable.

LORRAINE Oh, please stop. I hate when you pussyfoot around like that—It makes me feel guilty for no reason. You have been living in this house for six months. You are just as much a part of it as me or Bill or, to a much lesser extent, my husk of a mother in the other room.

LJUBA No, is your house, I am an employee.

LORRAINE I don't want to fight you on this dear, you're a darling and very accommodating but you need to feel absolutely at home here with us. Isn't that right, Bill? (*beat*) Bill? (*beat*) Bill! Do you feel like contributing something?

He looks up—

BILL I pay for everything in this house.

LORRAINE And we all appreciate that, you're very generous, but I meant contributing something to the *conversation*.

BILL Oh.

He looks back down to eat and read.

LORRAINE That's just lovely. Marriage is eternal and it gets better everyday.

Ljuba stifles a laugh which prompts Lorraine to crack as well, just as—

Bill has an attack. It feels like electricity is running down his spine. He tenses as it surges through him.

BILL Shit!

LORRAINE Bill—

BILL (*gritted teeth*) Motherfucker, motherfucker Jesus!

Lorraine abruptly stands up—she can't bear to see this. She walks to the fridge and adjusts magnets, humming to herself to avoid hearing Bill.

Ljuba, unfazed, walks to Bill and gently puts her hand on his shoulder.

Bill's body shivers as the pain runs through his body. The whole thing lasts about ten seconds.

Finally, he relaxes, but is now depressed.

Well, I'm finished for the night.

LORRAINE Oh, boo! Stay here, Bill. Stay downstairs!

BILL I'm going to sleep.

LORRAINE It's not even eight o'clock.

Bill checks his watch.

LJUBA Do you need help getting upstairs?

BILL No. Thank you, Ljuba.

LJUBA Yes, of course, Mr. Bill.

As Bill trudges up the stairs:

LORRAINE I love when she calls you Mr. Bill! It sounds like you're a children's cartoon character, doesn't it, Bill? *The Adventures of Mr. Bill and His Dog, Cracker. When we last left them, Mr. Bill was stuck in a time warp and Cracker was flying back to Earth to get help!*

Lorraine flits to the bottom of the stairs and calls after him:

You see? Reading about the Civil War, going to sleep at eight. It's starting! Goodnight, Old Man! Goodnight!

Bill grunts. Lorraine chokes up, her voice cracking:

Have I upset you, Bill? I would die if I've upset you.

BILL I'm not upset.

LORRAINE I'll be up in an hour. I love you sweetheart, I'll be up soon.

BILL Take your time.

LORRAINE I love you.

When he's gone:

He's getting worse.

LJUBA No, he is just tired, is all.

LORRAINE I stressed him out.

LJUBA No, stop. He's in pain. You were great.

LORRAINE You think so?

LJUBA Yes, yes! You are always great.

Lorraine nods, agreeing.

LORRAINE How?

LJUBA You make everything into something happy. I watch you: is like magic. Someone say something sad or angry and you just pretend like what they say is happy. Is like you don't even hear them sometimes. Is a gift, in some way.

LORRAINE Well, I do try to keep things lighthearted.

LJUBA And you do! You keep everything so lighthearted!

LORRAINE Last night, I caught him clutching the side of the bed while he was sleeping, like he was trying to crawl away from me. Even when he's sleeping, now, it's like he's repulsed by me.

LJUBA Maybe he had some kind of bad dream.

LORRAINE Bill's too unimaginative to have dreams.

LJUBA Did you talk about taking the pill again?

LORRAINE He refuses to take it.

LJUBA There's no side effect. Very little.

LORRAINE He thinks it's gauche to talk about erectile dysfunction and even worse to treat it like it's a legitimate medical condition.

LJUBA Maybe you hide it in his applesauce?

LORRAINE That's very cute.

LJUBA Thank you.

LORRAINE He used to fall asleep squeezing me from behind. I actually found it suffocating, his breathing in my ear, my nose— whatever he ate during the day, *assaulting* me throughout the night. I had to wait until he was fully asleep to extricate myself from his grip. There was almost something violent about the whole affair. But this is worse.

LJUBA I'm sorry, sweetheart.

LORRAINE Thank you, darling.

LJUBA You know, the last months that my husband and me live together, he sleeps on the floor in the kitchen.

LORRAINE What? You never told me that. Why?

LJUBA He don't want to sleep next to me.

LORRAINE You didn't have a couch?

LJUBA He say, "You too happy, Ljuba. Even when you sleep, is a bother to me."

LORRAINE The crime of too much happiness!

LJUBA Yes, "You too happy, Ljuba. You too much energy. You move too much. Is not normal."

LORRAINE Happy *and* moving? You should be ashamed of yourself.

LJUBA He tell me that it is more painful to sleep next to me than to sleep on the hard kitchen floor.

LORRAINE My god.

LJUBA Yes, is not nice.

They stew in their own worlds.

LORRAINE This is why I love talking to you. Anything sad in my life is automatically sadder in yours.

LJUBA I can make a list for you, you know, of everything sad in my life.

LORRAINE Yeah, would you do that for me?

LJUBA Yes of course. I will make some of it up, just to make you feel better.

LORRAINE Great, I wouldn't know the difference anyway.

There's a sweet pause—

I find you absolutely charming.

LJUBA And I find you charming.

LORRAINE Well, that's different. I'm *actively* charming. You're more *natural.*

LJUBA Can I—may I sit down?

LORRAINE Don't ask me that! It makes me feel weird. What am I, an emperor? I have a house. Just sit!

LJUBA Sorry, is a stupid habit.

Ljuba sits and they stare at each other for a moment.

Lorraine?

LORRAINE Yes.

LJUBA Do you think I have an accent?

LORRAINE An accent?

Suddenly, we hear the beep coming from the other room.

LJUBA   Oh, excuse me, Lorraine.

LORRAINE   Do you really have to go in there? She just buzzes you because she wants attention.

LJUBA   No, could be something wrong. I'm coming, Ruthie!

It beeps again.

LORRAINE   She's coming, Jesus Mom!

Ljuba exits into the bedroom.

LJUBA (*os*)   Okay, Ruthie, your head just fall to the side—it's okay Lorraine, her head just fall to the side.

LORRAINE   Well straighten it out and get back in here.

LJUBA (*os*)   Okay, I am!

Lorraine can't bear to be alone. She becomes agitated:

LORRAINE   Ljuba, I'm literally alone here!

LJUBA (*os*)   I'm coming!

Ljuba reenters.

Sorry. Her head just fall to the side.

LORRAINE   She was always very flexible. Now where were we?

LJUBA   Okay, yes—(*sits and takes a breath*) yes—do you know Carolina?

LORRAINE   Who?

LJUBA   The woman who works at Romero's.

LORRAINE   What's Romero's?

LJUBA   Romero's. I get food from there every week.

LORRAINE   The Italian place?

LJUBA Yes, Romero's. I walk there every week—two, three times a week. Is ten minutes away.

LORRAINE I never knew what it was called. The food shows up on my table by the grace of God for all I know, and I eat it.

LJUBA Anyway, Carolina is the woman who works there. The wife of Romero.

LORRAINE Oh, yes! I do know her. With the lazy eye.

LJUBA What is this?

LORRAINE A lazy eye? Her eye is like—(*indicates a lazy eye*)

LJUBA Oh, yes. There is something wrong there. Anyway, I go into Romero's for the past six month I work here. I maybe am in there one hundred times total, I don't know.

LORRAINE Jesus, really? Maybe we need to start switching it up.

LJUBA Is the only place with good food I can walk to.

LORRAINE Okay, fine—so what happened?

LJUBA So I always have a nice talk with Carolina. You know, nothing very special. How are you, I am good, what you buy, is it raining, you know.

LORRAINE Scintillating.

LJUBA And today, is nothing different. I buy normal thing, what you like, what Bill like, and as I pay for it, she say to me, Ljuba, where you from? I say, what? She say again, where you from? I tell her, here, I live ten minutes away. And she look at me weird. She make some strange face—

LORRAINE Because of the lazy eye—

LJUBA No, like she is *thinking* about me. Is unusual look, I can't describe it, I can feel it. And my heart is start racing, you know? I tell her again, I live ten minutes away. Is why I walk here. And she look

14

at me again. She say nothing. I say nothing. So I make a little joke, I say I am lucky I live so close to you and Romero, such good cooks.

LORRAINE That's not really a joke.

LJUBA And I walk out. And I can't breathe.

LORRAINE I don't understand.

LJUBA How she knows I'm not from here? How she knows I'm not born here, live here my whole life?

LORRAINE Are you serious?

LJUBA Yes, how she knows?

LORRAINE Sweetheart, don't take this the wrong way, but you couldn't seem more foreign if you had a Serbian flag tattooed on your forehead.

LJUBA So you think I have an accent?

LORRAINE Do I *think*?

LJUBA Yes. When I talk, can you hear an accent?

LORRAINE Honey, when you talk, it sounds like your mouth is full of marbles and peanut butter. It's only because I've done accent work myself that I can understand you. Did you really think you sound like the rest of us?

LJUBA I really did.

LORRAINE That's unbelievable to me.

LJUBA I thought I sounded close.

Ljuba sits, despondent.

LORRAINE Oh, come on, honey. Are you upset?

LJUBA I am.

LORRAINE I hope it wasn't because of anything I said.

LJUBA No, is not you, Lorraine.

LORRAINE I didn't think so.

LJUBA Is the *world*. Is like it is getting *meaner*, in some way. I can feel it. Like regular people, like this Carolina, she feel like she can think about me this way.

LORRAINE Do you want me to go in there and talk to her?

LJUBA And say what?

LORRAINE I don't know. That woman's face is a canvas of mistakes, we could literally say anything to make her feel terrible.

LJUBA And then what? She make one telephone call—"there is woman here with no papers, she come in here every week"—I go to jail. You see what I mean?
  I can't drive a car. I can't go to doctor, if I get sick. I can't take a bus, go to the airport, talk to a policeman like everyone else. I can't even see my daughter. And every single person—people like this woman—they can take my life in one second.

LORRAINE (*pause as she reflects on Ljuba's plight*) I hope it's not insensitive to say that it kind of reminds me of my own life.

LJUBA What do you mean?

LORRAINE In a different way of course, but you're kind of like me. Like you're always having to play a character. It's interesting.

LJUBA No. No, is not interesting.

LORRAINE Okay, so what do you wanna do? You're not planning on leaving us, are you?

LJUBA Do you remember I tell you about that man in Crown Heights? Juri?

LORRAINE I don't.

LJUBA You don't remember? I tell you he wants thirty thousand dollars to marry me.

16

LORRAINE Oh, vaguely.

LJUBA I was saving up thirty thousand dollars to marry Juri, you know, to get my papers, but some other woman come—she's not a nice woman, I know her, no one likes her—but she have the thirty thousand and he marry her first. And she gets a green card, I guess. Is easy. She bring her family over here, probably.

LORRAINE So what? You miss Juri? I'm sure there are other men who'd love to extort and marry you—

LJUBA All Serbian men who are American, they want thirty thousand dollars to marry. Is all the same. Unmarried Serbian man— could be fat, could be old, could be stupid—is like gold.

LORRAINE So, what, you want to get married?

LJUBA I need to. I get married—my life is suddenly normal. I go shopping, I drive, I bring my daughter here—

LORRAINE So what do you want from me? You need money? We honestly don't have anything between Bill's medical payments—

LJUBA I don't want more money. I just—you know so many people. And so many people love you.

LORRAINE Right, right.

LJUBA So I just want to know if you know any man who might marry me for the money I *do* have.

LORRAINE Well, how much do you have?

LJUBA I have half. I have fifteen thousand.

LORRAINE Okay, well maybe we can find you half a man. I married half a man. He's upstairs reading about Appomattox.

LJUBA Lorraine, is a serious problem!

LORRAINE And I'm trying to stay on task! Do you really have fifteen thousand dollars? I thought you send everything back to your daughter.

LJUBA I send *most* of my money back but I save a lot for this purpose exactly. For three years, I'm saving up.

LORRAINE You have fifteen thousand dollars? Where the hell do you keep that much money? In the mattress?

LJUBA The box spring.

LORRAINE The box spring? Are you serious?

LJUBA Yes, of course. Why is so surprising?

LORRAINE I just didn't think anyone actually puts money in a mattress. It's like you're Jan Val Jean hiding his loaf of bread from the gendarmes. It's so dramatic!

LJUBA Lorraine, you please maybe stay focus.

LORRAINE Sorry darling. I thought I was staying focus!

LJUBA Is okay.

LORRAINE I'm sure I can find you someone.

LJUBA Really?

LORRAINE This is exactly what I do! I bring people together!

LJUBA You know is not such an easy job. We have to look like we really married. Have pictures of the wedding, have pictures of vacation, of friends. We must have one bank account, gas bill, everything, pretend we live together.

LORRAINE I know all about it.

LJUBA How?

LORRAINE Darling, I'm an artist. We live in the shadows, we bend the rules. Now I want you to stop worrying. I will take care of everything.

LJUBA My god, thank you Lorraine.

LORRAINE I'll start making calls tomorrow.

LJUBA Okay, but you know, you can't tell so many people about this. It's not perfectly legal.

LORRAINE You don't think I can keep a secret?

LJUBA I don't know. You enjoy talking so much.

LORRAINE I am a natural performer. But your secret is as safe as money in a mattress!

LJUBA Oh, Lorraine, thank you!

Ljuba swings her arms around Lorraine.

LORRAINE Don't thank me! It's my pleasure. I'm like Yenta the Matchmaker, a role I could have devoured if I weren't too pretty when they did it in town. (*beat*) Can I tell you something?

LJUBA Of course.

LORRAINE I sometimes fantasize about when it's just the two of us.

LJUBA What do you mean?

LORRAINE Well, my mother's not going to live forever and Bill's not in such great shape. At some point, it'll just be the two of us left. Two little monkeys jumping on the bed.

LJUBA And what will we do all day? If is just the two of us?

LORRAINE For starters, we'll repaint the house—

LJUBA What color?

LORRAINE Any color. It's so drab in here, don't you think?

LJUBA And what else?

LORRAINE Maybe we'll get a pool.

LJUBA Ha! A pool?

LORRAINE Nothing too crazy, but just something to sit by. We don't even have to swim in it. I just want to sit near a pool with a glass of something in my hand. Two gorgeous women sitting poolside, I like the image. I like what it represents.

LJUBA   Yes, I like this too.

LORRAINE   And you know what I think would be great?

LJUBA   What?

LORRAINE   I think we should build a little stage over here. Just a platform, really, nothing extravagant, just something for us to perform. Mark from the theater is very handy. And you're actually a very good actress. You don't give yourself enough credit.

LJUBA   Oh stop it.

LORRAINE   I won't stop it. You are very good. When we were running lines yesterday, you teared up when you were saying goodbye to Liat. I saw it. You almost cried.

LJUBA   Did I?

LORRAINE   Yes. It's probably because your life is so sad. You're very easily shaken.

LJUBA   . . . Okay.

LORRAINE   And of course we'll do all of our own plays!

LJUBA   Ooh, I love this.

LORRAINE   Great, so what should we start with?

LJUBA   Maybe a ballet?

LORRAINE   A ballet! Yes! So classy. Who would you play?

LJUBA (*thinks*)   I would play a young woman—three men are in love with me.

LORRAINE   You little vixen!

LJUBA   And I don't love any of them.

LORRAINE   Picky!

LJUBA My heart is only for the young prince. Who lives in the castle.

LORRAINE A gold digger. I love it.

LJUBA And the prince, he also love me.

LORRAINE Of course he does. Look at you.

LJUBA But he's marry to an evil woman.

LORRAINE The princess.

LJUBA The witch.

LORRAINE Oh.

LJUBA Yes, he married to the witch.

LORRAINE I don't know why a prince would be married to a witch, but okay.

LJUBA And the witch keep the prince locked up in the castle.

LORRAINE Sure.

LJUBA So I have to rescue him.

LORRAINE It's like you're four years old, coming up with this stuff. I love it.

LJUBA And so I . . . (*thinking*) . . . Yes! I use the three men to help me. Because they are truly in love with me so they will do anything for me. Even if is to help me find a different man.

LORRAINE A twist ending! Very interesting. I love a good twist!

LJUBA Thank you.

LORRAINE And who do I play?

LJUBA Do you know how to do ballet?

LORRAINE I could figure it out.

21

LJUBA Because I've been study since I am six years old in Novi Sad.

LORRAINE It's my stage. I need a role.

LJUBA I guess you could be the witch.

LORRAINE The witch! Do you think I could be a witch?

We hear a beep from offstage.

LJUBA Oh, excuse me Lorraine.

LORRAINE Wait a second—do you really think I could be a witch?

LJUBA I think you are a great actress, Lorraine. You could play any role.

LORRAINE (*mulls it over*) That's true. I'd probably humanize the witch in some way. Okay. That's our first show. A ballet about a witch!

LJUBA Perfect!

LORRAINE First we get you married and then we do the witch ballet. You see? You're crying one moment and giddy the next. That's what I do for you. That's what we do for each other.

Beep beep beep.

LJUBA Okay Ruthie! I'm coming! I was just in the bathroom!

Ljuba begins to head off to the bedroom—

LORRAINE Look at you—a little schoolgirl waiting for a dance, looking for a schoolboy who will give her a chance . . .

Ljuba giddily exits into the bedroom.

Lorraine is left alone. She tries out some ballet moves and begins humming "Twin Soliloquies" from South Pacific.

Lights fade as the official recording of "Twin Soliloquies" takes over and plays through the following transition—

SCENE 2

A week later, around the same time.

Bill sits in his La-Z-Boy, nursing his scotch.

After a moment, the doorbell rings.

LORRAINE (*os*) He's here! Bill, he's here!

Lorraine enters from upstairs.

I really ask for so little, Bill. I'm just asking you to be nice to the
young man. I know it's painful for you, but this is such an important
night for me.

The doorbell rings again—

Please just promise me you'll try to be pleasant.

BILL I'm not promising anything.

LORRAINE Bill, please.

BILL My back hurts.

LORRAINE God damnit!

*He goes back to his book. Lorraine psychs herself up and opens the door
with practiced panache.*

Well, hello there, Lootellan!

*RONNY (40, Asian American) enters, dressed respectfully in a blazer
and jeans. He is sweetly effeminate.*

RONNY Oh, I must be at the wrong house—I'm looking for a
French Planter—I think he lives on top of the hill. Do you know him?

23

LORRAINE   French Planter?

RONNY   Yeah, name's Emile De Becque.

LORRAINE   All French Planter Stingy Bastards! But you sexy man.

RONNY (*laughing*)   And "scene"!

LORRAINE (*to Bill*)   That's our dialogue from the play, sweetie. Don't worry. I'm not hitting on him. And it wouldn't matter if I was anyway. Ronny is as gay as the day is long. Well, not your days, Bill, you wake up at noon. (*to Ronny*) How are you sweetums? Thank you so much for coming by.

RONNY   Seeing you six days a week just wasn't enough!

LORRAINE   Have you met my husband, Bill? Bill, this is Lootellan Joseph Cable.

RONNY   Reporting for duty! Nice to meet you, sir. I'm Ronny— *playing* Lieutenant Cable opposite Lorraine's brilliant Bloody Mary.

LORRAINE   What's great about having Ronny in the cast is that he's able to give us insight into the exotic Asian experience.

RONNY   Actually, I was born and raised Cleveland.

LORRAINE   Oh, don't be so modest! You know, I'd love to pick your brain at some point for Mary's backstory.

RONNY   I don't think you need any help, Lorraine. (*to Bill*) She's doing just wonderfully in the show.

BILL   She's doing good?

RONNY   Good? Are you kidding? She's a genius. Even in rehearsals.

LORRAINE   Well I like to rehearse at show level, always have. Keeps everybody on their toes, especially our fearless leader, James Peter, who's a brilliant director but lets people coast through rehearsals and is shocked when they struggle to reach the back row during performances.

RONNY   Paging Kelly DeSanto!

LORRAINE   Donne moi your accoutrement!

RONNY   Thank you so much. I have to admit, I'm a little nervous.

Lorraine removes Ronny's scarf and heads off to hang it. Ronny finds himself alone with Bill and awkwardly sings:

I don't know why I'm frightened!

LORRAINE   And don't mind Bill. He's just eating his dinner. He has to eat at the same time every night because he takes a handful of pills, none of which seem to work, for depression and multiple sclerosis. Although, he'd appreciate if you didn't tell the cast or JP about it because it's a private family matter.

RONNY   I'm sorry to hear that, Bill. You . . . you look totally fine, I wouldn't have suspected anything. I actually have an aunt with MS.

LORRAINE   Do you? And how is she doing?

RONNY (*remembers she's dead*)   Um, well . . . she's . . . actually. You know, I haven't—

LORRAINE   She sounds interesting!
Ljuba!
Sorry about this, Ronny, your lady-in-waiting is just primping, she'll be out in a minute. (*Sings to Ljuba*) Winnifred, Winnifred, Winnifred! Where do you think you are?! Girl from the swamps!
Ljuba!

LJUBA (*os*)   I'm coming Lorraine.

Ljuba comes out—she has dolled herself up.

LORRAINE   Va va vook! Hey there, supermodel! What did you do with that drab nurse I usually see moping around the house?

LJUBA   That ugly woman? I told her to leave the house—tonight is special!

LORRAINE   Okay, well just make sure she's back in time for dinner.

RONNY   Hi there, Ljuba. I'm Ronny. (*sings*) I've heard so much about you.

LJUBA   Thank you, Ronny. I'm sorry I kept you waiting. My stupid hair—

LORRAINE   *Look at those big black eyes just staring out of her beautiful face!* Sorry! That's from the play! I have to stop doing that! Are you okay sweetie?

LJUBA   A little nervous maybe.

RONNY   I was literally just saying the same thing.

LJUBA   Really?

RONNY   I didn't think I would be—

LJUBA   Yes, me too, but is such a strange situation, in a way.

RONNY   Exactly.

LORRAINE   Well, don't be nervous, either one of you cute little things. I will be with both of you every step of the way. Now, let's sit down and get to know each other. I bought an assortment of cookies and cakes, which Ronny and I will have to work off by opening night, lest we be upstaged by our own thighs. And I think Ljuba wanted to open a bottle of some of her Serbian magic potion.

LJUBA   Ah, yes, wine is okay for you, Ronny?

RONNY   I'm not old enough to drink! I'm kidding, it sounds delicious.

LORRAINE   It's not, but it reminds her of home. Get the red, sweetheart. It tastes less like ammonia.

Ljuba grabs a bottle of red wine and prepares three glasses.

LJUBA (*trying to impress*)   This is from the northern region of Serbia, near the Hungarian border. Is an area called Vojvodina. Is Serbia but

26

the accent and the culture is more like Hungary, is very refined. My family comes from a farm not so many kilometers from where this wine comes from.

RONNY How wonderful, it's like a vacation in a glass.

LJUBA Yes, exactly.

RONNY Now I could tell everybody that I've been to Serbia!

LJUBA Isn't wine the most fun way to travel?

RONNY Of course! You avoid all the jet lag!

LORRAINE You two are precious.

LJUBA Mr. Bill, I can pour you a glass?

BILL No.

LORRAINE Oh come on Bill. Have a little sip, we're celebrating! It's like we're on a double date!

BILL No thank you, Ljuba.

LJUBA Of course.

LORRAINE Sit down, sit down. You're making me dizzy.

LJUBA Oh, sorry, Lorraine.

LORRAINE That's okay, honey. So this all started when I spotted Ronny across the crowded rehearsal room and somehow I knew—"I knew even then!"—that he'd be perfect. Isn't that right, Ronny? He was my first and only choice.

RONNY Yeah, not to be immediately, like *money hungry*, but when Lorraine mentioned this opportunity I just breathed this huge sigh of relief. You see, Steven—that's my partner—was always the breadwinner and he's been out of work for the past year.

LJUBA I'm so sorry Ronny.

RONNY   Oh, it's not your fault, sweetie. AT&T had massive layoffs, across the whole state, really.

LORRAINE (*mock surprised*)   And you guys can't get by on your salary from *South Pacific*? (*stage-whispered to Ljuba*) *We don't get paid anything.*

RONNY   That's right. Lorraine's right, it's all for the love, which is another problem because Steven's been putting more pressure on me to spend my time doing something a little more . . . "practical," I suppose.

LORRAINE   You see, I'm lucky, though, because Bill's supportive of the arts and has a generous pension.

RONNY   Yeah, and unfortunately *we* have a landlord who's straight out of *Oliver Twist*. I feel like I'm always groveling with him: (*in a British orphan voice*) *Please sir, can I have another month?*

Lorraine and Ronny laugh.

LJUBA   And Lorraine told you that we have to be married for at least three years? Your partner, he is okay with this?

RONNY   Oh yes, absolutely. I'm all yours! Steven will never get married. He thinks gay marriage "whitewashes our struggle"—or something! I'm not really sure! *I'd* be fine getting married—Steven's the political one and I'm the romantic. He's always marching for something or signing a petition. And I'm always like, "Can you save the world a little quicker please! My casserole's getting cold!"

LORRAINE   Okay, maybe don't mention casseroles when you're trying to seem straight in front of the immigration officers.

RONNY   What about references to old musicals?

LORRAINE   Yes, if they say "*Oh! . . .*"

RONNY   I'll try not to say "*—Klahoma! Where the wind comes sweeping down the plain! Where the waving wheat sure smells sweet, when the wind comes right behind the rain."*

They all chuckle.

LJUBA Wow, you have a beautiful voice.

RONNY Gosh, thanks. That wasn't serious. But, if you want, I'd be happy to sing for you at some point. I could do my whole cabaret show—

LJUBA Oh my, I would love this.

LORRAINE There's a solid hour about how his dad didn't 'get' him.

RONNY Shut up, Lorraine.

LJUBA No, that sounds interesting.

RONNY You are just too sweet. And I should also say that Lorraine told me about your situation, about what your life is like and that you want to bring your daughter over here. To be honest, it's something you read about in the news and kind of disregard. But I just really felt for you.

LJUBA Thank you.

RONNY And I remember my dad telling me that someone threw a glass bottle at his head two weeks after he landed in the States.

LJUBA My goodness. I'm so sorry, Ronny.

RONNY The world can be vicious.

LJUBA When I first get here, my landlord in Queens called me the Soviet whore.

RONNY Jesus. Wait—you're not even from the Soviet Union, are you?

LJUBA Yes, also I'm not a whore.

RONNY (*laughing*) Ah, yes! Also there's that!

LJUBA Yes, also there is that!

RONNY Well, Steven's parents still call me "oriental." And I'm always like, "I'm not a throw pillow, thank you very much!" People can be so stupid.

LJUBA Yes, maybe is stupid, but also, sometimes I think people just don't know about the world. Is not their fault, always, maybe. Or sometimes, I think, a person's life can be so good that they don't even know that they are so lucky.

RONNY Hmm.

LORRAINE Bill had an aunt at Auschwitz.

We hear a beep from the other room. Ljuba's being called.

Ah, Jesus. Great timing as usual, Mom! That's my mother, she's in the other room.

RONNY Oh, right, of course.

LJUBA Ronny, would you mind if I went in for one minute? I'm sure is nothing.

Beep—

I'm sorry, Lorraine. I'll be very quick.

LORRAINE Don't worry about us, honey, go go go! And we promise not to talk about you!

Lorraine does a showy 'wink' at Ronny for Ljuba's benefit.

LJUBA I'm coming Ruthie! I was just in the bathroom—

When Ljuba's gone:

LORRAINE Isn't she just great?

RONNY She is. Very sweet.

LORRAINE I told you.

RONNY Do I seem like a blithering idiot?

LORRAINE Usually. But not tonight. You can be very charming when you want to be.

RONNY Really? I feel like I'm rambling.

Ljuba appears—

LJUBA   She just needs I change her diaper.

LORRAINE   Take your time—wash your hands!

Ljuba exits back into the bedroom.

You should see her with my mother. She's a wonder. I mean, my mother provides nothing—zip—but Ljuba continues to take care of her with such grace. It's almost like she really cares.

RONNY   That's so selfless.

LORRAINE   Well she really has no other choice but, yes, it is. And it's so nice to be able to have my mother here. Most people just ship their parents off to a warehouse somewhere—

RONNY   Oh yeah, Steven's parents are both in places like that—separate ones, actually!

LORRAINE   And it's just horrible, all due respect. No one touches them. No one talks to them. It's horrid the way we treat the elderly in this society. But Ljuba—she's just incredible. She actually sleeps in the room with her. Can you imagine?

RONNY   Oh my God.

LJUBA (*os*)   Okay, I'm coming back. Sorry about this.

Ljuba reenters. They stare at her with new adoration.

RONNY   Sooo . . . where were we?

LORRAINE   You guys were getting fake married for a green card—

RONNY   Ha ha. No, Ljuba, I think you were about to tell me about what you wanted to do after you get citizenship.

LORRAINE   I already told you, she wants to bring her daughter over here.

RONNY   Yes, but what about you?

31

LJUBA   What do you mean?

RONNY   I mean what do *you* want to do when you have citizenship?

LORRAINE   Bringing her child to the richest country on Earth isn't enough?

LJUBA   I want to be a pharmacist.

RONNY   Really?

LORRAINE   What?

LJUBA   Yes, back in Serbia, I was study to be a pharmacist and I get very close, one year away when I get pregnant with my daughter. So my husband—my *ex*-husband—he asked me to stop—

LORRAINE   And then he left her for a hooker. Can you believe that?

LJUBA   Lorraine!

RONNY   My goodness, is that true?

LJUBA (*chuckling bashfully*)   Is not fully true, no—

LORRAINE   A hooker with a bad perm! Sorry! Ljuba showed me a picture of her online. The only thing worse than a hooker is a hooker with a bad perm! I mean, just from a business standpoint . . .

LJUBA   And I want to move to Florida.

LORRAINE   Florida? What the hell is in Florida?

LJUBA   It looks like a beautiful place, I don't know. I always just think: *One day, I will live in Florida.*

LORRAINE   You don't want to live in Florida. Everyone dies there!

LJUBA   No, I look at pictures. I mean, since a long time ago, back in Serbia, I become, like, obsess with Florida. Everyone knows this about me. Florida is like a strange shape of a state and so—

LORRAINE   I bet Ronny likes the shape of Florida!

RONNY Are you twelve years old?

LORRAINE I'm young at heart.

LJUBA I mean, it is a strange shape because wherever you live, if it is in Florida, it is near to the water. This is what makes it such an unusual state in America. Serbia is stuck in the middle of Europe.

LORRAINE You never told me any of this—

LJUBA You never ask me.

LORRAINE You can't move away from me. What about my mother?

LJUBA It's not happening tomorrow.

LORRAINE I don't care when it's happening.

RONNY Settle down, girls!

LJUBA (*laughing at the thought*) You think that, when I bring my daughter here, we all going to live in the same house?

LORRAINE Yes! What's wrong with that? Of course I thought you'd live with me. We were gonna have a little theater and swimming pool. But now, suddenly you're moving across the country because there's some water and a state shaped like a phallus!

RONNY Well, I'm sure she'll visit you Lorraine, right Ljuba?

LJUBA Yes, of course. I visit you every chance I get.

LORRAINE (*backing off*) Okay, okay! I'm just worried about you, sweetie. (*to Ronny*) I'm just worried about her. She'd fall completely apart without me.

RONNY Wouldn't we all!

LORRAINE She's smart in some ways, don't get me wrong. But the world eats people like her for breakfast.

LJUBA Well then is a good thing because breakfast is the most important meal of the day.

They all chuckle.

LORRAINE   I taught her that.

RONNY   And why do you wanna be a pharmacist?

LJUBA   I love every part of it. People think we just sort the pills into different bottles, but is so much more. We must know about each individual patient. For example, if someone takes a medicine for the blood pressure, they cannot just take blood thinning medicine. You see?

RONNY   Why, they conflict?

LJUBA   Not conflict, but is possible that they add up to too much of the same problem. Blood pressure medicine makes your blood thin. So if the blood is too thin *and* you are also taking the blood thinner *and* you get a cut—even a little cut, it maybe seems like no problem—you could die. So is important that the pharmacist know about each individual. Could mean life or death.

RONNY   Of course. My goodness.

LORRAINE   Well, all that information is on computers now, isn't it, Ljuba? So you don't really have to know about it anymore. Because it's on computers.

LJUBA   It's maybe on computers, Lorraine, but I think it's also important for a real human being to be there.

RONNY   That's exactly what I think!

LORRAINE   Well I think you both sound like Pollyanna. I trust a computer *far* more than a person to take care of me! But I think we've strayed far enough off topic for one night, don't you? We have a marriage to create!

RONNY   Sure, sorry, I'm just babbling!

LJUBA   Yes, sorry, me too.

LORRAINE   That's okay. It's normal when you first meet someone. You're both desperate to make a good impression but I know you guys already so I don't have that problem. Should we talk money?

RONNY Uh, awkward!

LORRAINE Someone had to say it. Ljuba has been dutifully saving fifteen thousand dollars—in cash! And—Bill, plug your ears!—she's hiding it in the least conspicuous place in the house. (*gestures to the bedroom*)

LJUBA Lorraine, please—

LORRAINE You're giving it to him anyway! So how should she pay you?

RONNY Honestly, Steven's the money guy. He's figuring out a way to set up an escrow box . . . or checking deposit . . . account to hold the blah, blah, blah, I don't know! It's all Greek to me! He said it should be set up by next week.

LJUBA Okay, is fine. I pay you next week.

RONNY Great! Now let's never talk about that again!

LJUBA Yes, that's a great idea! And I will speak to my lawyer tomorrow about everything I must do. But I promise I will not bore you with all of the details. I will only speak to Steven the Money Guy!

LORRAINE God! Aren't you just the *cutest*! It's a good thing he's gay and I'm on a diet because we would just eat you up!

LJUBA (*mock scared*) Oh no!

LORRAINE This is all just going so well! Bill, isn't this all just going so well? Now that we're all agreed on the terms, I think we're ready for the fun part!

RONNY Whoops! I've been having fun the whole time.

LJUBA Oh, me too. Whoops!

LORRAINE Since you're supposed to have pictures that show the progression of your relationship, I dug out my old Hasselblad!

Lorraine pulls out an old camera.

I've been looking for an excuse to use this old thing.

RONNY Oh my gosh, Lorraine, I look like a mess.

LORRAINE You look great, stop it! And we're not taking headshots, you're just meeting your wife! Doesn't he look great, Ljuba?

LJUBA Yes, he looks very handsome.

RONNY Well, thank you, "wife."

LJUBA You're welcome, "husband."

LORRAINE Perfect, now get closer together. And hold up your wine. Smile!

The couple, laughing, gets closer and holds up their wine glasses.

LORRAINE Ronny you look gay, don't smile so big!

Ronny does a closed mouth smile.

LORRAINE Okay, better. You look like such a sweet couple. It doesn't even look weird that he's Asian!
Now stand up for a casual one, like you're just meeting and having a conversation.

LJUBA What do you mean?

LORRAINE Just turn to each other. Like you're talking at a party.

They turn to each other but immediately feel uncomfortable. Ljuba laughs.

LJUBA Uh . . .

RONNY What should we talk about?

LORRAINE It doesn't matter, it's a picture. Just say anything. Talk! Go!

RONNY (*cutely formal*) Hello. How are you doing?

LJUBA (*cutely mirroring him*) I am doing good. Thank you sir.

RONNY My name is Ronny. I feel like a robot.

LJUBA My name is Ljuba. I feel like robot too.

LORRAINE   Okay, most of that is unusable. All right, now it's my turn. I should be in a few.

LJUBA   Are you trying take my man away, Lorraine?

LORRAINE   Ooh! Is someone jealous? Bill, she's jealous! What are you gonna do about it?

Bill looks up, irritated that he's being referenced.

Seriously, I should probably be in a few.

RONNY   Why?

LORRAINE   I don't know. I'm like the best friend. What? You don't have any friends? It looks weird.

RONNY   So who would take it?

LORRAINE   Bill! Bill, can you take a few shots of us?

BILL   What?

LORRAINE   We're taking pictures. To show them as a couple in different situations.

BILL   Okay?

LORRAINE   And I have to be in a few, so I need you to take the picture.

BILL   Why do you have to be in the picture?

LORRAINE   Because I'm the linchpin! I'm the doting mother figure, who's been trying to set them up for years. Ronny, over here, is the consummate bachelor, always bragging about all the women he's slept with but deep inside he just wants a nice woman to settle down with—

RONNY   Sounds like someone's thought a lot about her character—

LORRAINE   I do it instinctively! And Ljuba's the quiet foreigner who's always getting hit on by the worst men! She goes on nightmare blind date after nightmare blind date, just wanting to meet

37

an honest guy who likes her for more than just a roll around in the hay. And I'm Geppetto! I'm Cupid! Secretly pulling the strings in the background, waiting for Ronny to finish sowing his wild oats and Ljuba to realize that looks aren't everything. I've been circling these two for years and I finally found the perfect opportunity to pounce. This is *my* moment, Bill, goddamnit, and I need you to take a picture!

BILL I'm not taking a picture.

LORRAINE Okay, then which one of you knows how to use this kind of camera?

RONNY I think I might, I used to have something ancient like that!

LORRAINE Perfect! Ljuba, come here, we'll do a few posed to camera because I don't look great in profile.

Lorraine poses with Ljuba. Through smiles:

LJUBA So, this is just a picture of me and you?

LORRAINE Yes.

LJUBA So how does this help with the marriage?

LORRAINE I don't know. It's like a picture of the *night*. Our fun night! The Three Amigos! Now let's do one back to back.

They pose back to back.

LORRAINE Ronny, do we look like sisters? I feel like we look like sisters!

RONNY Not really—

LORRAINE Oh, come on, Ronny! Use your imagination!

RONNY I mean, if anything, you look like mother and daughter.

LORRAINE Do we really? I love it!

LJUBA Take one of me hugging my mother!

Ljuba grabs Lorraine and hugs her.

LORRAINE   Hi Daughter!

LJUBA   Hi Mama!

LORRAINE   I love you my baby!

The women hug and smile toward camera when Lorraine, suddenly choked up, clutches Ljuba.

I love you my baby. I love you my baby!

LJUBA   Lorraine.

Lorraine doesn't respond, overcome with emotion.

LJUBA   Lorraine. I can't breathe.
I can't breathe. You're squeezing me so much.

LORRAINE   Oh! Sorry dear! Of course. (*snaps out of it*) Sorry about that! I got carried away.

RONNY   You know what? I actually *don't* know what I'm doing with this camera.

LORRAINE   Oh, Ronny!

RONNY   And also, I have to say, it just looks kind of weird here. Like we're just posing in a house for no reason. It doesn't feel real.

LJUBA   I'm sorry—I'm not such a good actress.

LORRAINE   I can change the backdrop—I have a kind of Chinese scarf in the basement—

RONNY   No—you know where we should probably go?

LORRAINE (*lighting up*)   Into the city?

RONNY   No, I was thinking that great little bar, where we did the last cast party, the one that's connected to the mall—

LORRAINE   Ruby Tuesday's?

RONNY Yeah, it has a nice atmosphere. The story could even be that Ljuba and I met there—on separate dates, with other people!

LJUBA Oh yes, this is interesting. Like we were on separate *bad* dates with other people.

RONNY Exactly. And when the people we were with went to the bathroom . . .

LJUBA This is when we notice each other.

RONNY Very romantic!

LJUBA Thank you! I was just going off what you were saying.

LORRAINE And who am I?

RONNY You could still be the cupid, I guess.

LORRAINE Not if you were on separate bad dates. I mean, in your version, I would be trying to set you guys up for years and then, *magically,* you wind up meeting in a completely unrelated way? It doesn't make any sense. *I* need to have set you up! Otherwise, your story is unbelievable and you're both gonna end up in prison! *If* you want to do the bar idea, I think it *has* to have a cast party element. Like it was a cast party for *Annie Get Your Gun*—I have some hats in the basement—and I brought my single friend, Ljuba, to meet my single friend Ronny, who was starring alongside my Annie Oakley as Chief Sitting Bull. That's the *only* way the bar idea would work!

RONNY I'd be good with that. Ljuba?

LJUBA Yes, of course. Lorraine strikes again with a brilliant idea!

RONNY I'd have to agree! So should I drive?

LORRAINE Perfect.

Lorraine begins heading off—

LJUBA Wait—Lorraine, you're coming too?

LORRAINE Yeah, of course.

LJUBA   So who is going to stay with your mother?

LORRAINE   Oh, shit. I forgot about her. Bill?

They all look to Bill, who is reading, and collectively disregard him.

RONNY   Lorraine, do you think you can just monitor her while we're at the bar?

LORRAINE   By myself?

RONNY   Isn't she your mother?

LORRAINE   Well, sure, technically.

RONNY   We'll be five minutes away.

LORRAINE   This is all happening so quickly. What do I say to her if she rings?

LJUBA   Just say, "Ljuba will be in the room soon. Relax, Ruthie. Relax, Ruthie." But you can call her "Mom."

LORRAINE   Do I have to go in there? Or can I kind of just yell it from out here?

LJUBA   Either is okay.

LORRAINE   This whole thing was my idea!

RONNY   And it was a great idea, Lorraine. Thank you so much. You're a lifesaver! *(in a cowboy voice)* I promise to have the little lady home before midnight!

Ronny kisses Lorraine on the cheeks and exits—

Ljuba lingers. Lorraine is deflated, but sincere. There is a calm tenderness to the following:

LJUBA   How do I look?

LORRAINE   You look gorgeous, of course. You always do.

Ljuba fluffs her hair.

41

LJUBA   My hair is flat—

LORRAINE   Your hair is fine.

Lorraine gently takes Ljuba's hands out of her hair. Ljuba grabs Lorraine's hands, tightly.

LJUBA   Lorraine. I want . . . I should thank you. I don't know what to say. You make my life . . . *possible*. Is such a good thing that you do.

LORRAINE   Of course, sweetheart.

LJUBA   I feel like a teenage girl! You're the best!

LORRAINE   Go get 'em, tiger.

Ljuba kisses her on both cheeks, exits. Lorraine gently closes the door. Bill stays reading.

Well that was nice. Young love.

Lorraine begins to clean up. She speaks half to herself, half to Bill.

I guess this is what it feels like to truly help those in need.

It's funny, I tend to think of myself as a kind of flighty artist, my head in the clouds, an eccentric. *That's just Lorraine. Don't bother Lorraine. She's an artist!*

And it's something I've come to terms with.

I never thought I'd help people in such a *direct* way. Saving a life, teaching a child how to read, feeding a hungry stomach. No. I always thought that my lot in life was to help people en masse. Through my work. People see me on stage. They see the human condition— it filters through me—and maybe they learn a little something about themselves. And if they've walked away with a new sense of understanding, of being able to look at their fellow man and not just see a husk, but a soul? Well then I've done my job.

Lorraine takes a sip of her wine—

Oh, how I wish I could spend my life on that stage, Bill. That my days were inverted, that I only had to spend two hours a night as Lorraine and I could spend the other twenty-two as Mary.

She pours herself some more wine—

The house is suddenly so quiet. (*fondly*) Ljuba.

She slowly ambles toward Bill—

Do you remember what you said to me when you saw me in *Miss
Saigon*?
  The scene where I go to Saigon and meet the girl in the hotel
room. And I see the child—my *husband's* child—and the girl pleads
with me, "Take him back. Let him have a normal life in America."
And I just can't do it. I refuse. "I want my *own* children," I tell her. "I
need to be selfish. I'm sorry." God, what a scene.
  And after our opening, I walked into the lobby, makeup still caked
to my face, sweat pouring down my blouse. And I saw you there,
holding the program, in your tweed blazer and clapping for me. You
were the only one in the lobby clapping.
  And you gave me the biggest hug. And I said, "I'm going to get
makeup on you!" But you hugged me even tighter.
  And do you remember what you said to me?
  You pulled me in and you whispered into my ear: "I saw myself."
  Do you remember that Bill?
  You said, "I saw myself up there. You allowed me to see myself."
  Do you remember that?

Bill looks up at her—

You do.

BILL   That was your best role.

LORRAINE   It was just a supporting character.

BILL   I still think it was your best.

*Lorraine sidles up to his chair and puts her body against his arm. They
are looking at each other.*

LORRAINE   Bill, have a sip of wine.

BILL   It gives me a headache.

LORRAINE   I'll massage your temples until you fall asleep.

BILL   You will?

LORRAINE   I'll massage your temples until it's morning.

She gently puts her glass to his lips. He takes a small sip.

I think you're going to like me in this role too.

She gives him another small sip. She walks around him and begins massaging his temples.

There is this moment in the show, Bill, where I'm trying to hawk a shrunken head to a soldier and everyone is laughing at me—I'm mispronouncing words, I'm aggressive, I'm a total buffoon.

And then, like lightning, there's a shift. The lights dim, the strings hum and I look out—I look out across the ocean to my home—a magical fantasy island in the distance. An electricity fills the air. You could hear a pin drop.

And, at this moment Bill, I could do *anything*. I have them in my hand. No one moves. I can hear it.

And I start to sing.

The audience is shocked at first. "Is this the same woman we've been watching for forty-five minutes? Is this the same woman who was our jester, our fool?"

And I sing out—with no humor, no affectation.

And I know that no one will ever see me the same way again.

Their laughter becomes sympathy.

The court jester becomes the queen.

That's what the theater can do—

Lorraine begins singing quietly to Bill. It is tender and calm and unusually sincere.

Most people live on a lonely island,
Lost in the middle of a foggy sea.
Most people long for another island,
One where they know they will like to be.

Bali Ha'i may call you,
Any night, any day,
In your heart, you'll hear it call you:
"Come away . . . come away."

    She hums the accompaniment and begins swaying to the music.

Bill. Stand up. Dance with me.

    She gives him another sip of wine.

BILL   I'm not dancing, Lorraine.

LORRAINE   Then stay where you are and just hold me.

    Lorraine presses her body into Bill's arms and sways against him.

Bali Ha'i will whisper
On the wind of the sea:
"Here am I, your special island!
Come to me, come to me!"

    Lights fade as Lorraine's singing gives way to the recording of "Bali Ha'i,"
    sung by Muriel Smith.

Your own special hopes,
Your own special dreams,
Bloom on the hillside
And shine in the streams.

    In near darkness, we see that Bill and Lorraine are gone.

    After a moment, something outside passes by the sliding glass doors. It's
    eerie.

    It passes by again. It's impossible to tell what it is. An animal? A burglar?
    The song continues:

If you try, you'll find me
Where the sky meets the sea.
Here am I your special island
Come to me, come to me.

Then, one of the glass doors begins to jiggle. A person becomes visible through the glass door.

The person is crouched down, trying to break into the house. They jiggle one of the doors until it pops. With the crescendo of the song, the door slides open and the person is visible in eerie silhouette.

Bali Ha'i,
Bali Ha'i,
Bali Ha'i!

It is a young woman shouldering a bike messenger bag.

She enters the house, looks around casually, and drops her bag on a chair.

She walks upstairs but just to take a peek.

Someday you'll see me, floatin' in the sunshine
My head stickin' out from a low-flying cloud
You'll hear me call you, singin' through the sunshine
Sweet and clear as can be.

She reenters and heads toward the fridge. She opens it and her face is finally illuminated.

This is JENNY (30). She grabs a bottle of water and begins heading toward Ruthie's bedroom.

Come to me, here am I, come to me . . .

If you try, you'll find me
Where the sky meets the sea
Here am I, your special island
Come to me, come to me.

Jenny slowly enters the bedroom of her grandmother.

Bali Ha'i,
Bali Ha'i,
Bali Ha'i!

The song ends and the house is still—

The front door slowly opens and Ljuba enters quietly.

She is a bit drunk and, though she's careful to not make a sound to wake Bill and Lorraine, she can't help but dance a little, giddy from her date.

She hums a pop song, shimmies to the freezer and takes out a microwave burrito. She rolls it in a paper towel and puts it in the microwave.

As it cooks, she dances to the song in her head, when she notices that the sliding glass door is open. She peers outside, in a panic—

She considers waking Lorraine but then decides to enter Ruthie's bedroom.

There is a moment of stillness and then Ljuba shrieks!

Suddenly, Ljuba runs in, chased out of the room by Jenny.

JENNY   Who the fuck are you? Who the fuck are you?

LJUBA   I—I—Lorraine!

JENNY   What the fuck are you doing here? Answer me!

LJUBA   I'm Ljuba—I take—

Ljuba is tongue-tied and flustered and cowering from fear as Jenny backs her up against the wall—

JENNY   What the fuck do you think you're doing here?

LORRAINE   Jenny? Jenny!

Lorraine appears. Without missing a beat, Jenny turns her aggression toward Lorraine.

JENNY   Who the fuck is she?

Suddenly, the microwave dings. There's a weird pause, which deflates the tension.

LJUBA   Ah, my burrito. Sorry—

JENNY   Who the fuck is she?

LORRAINE   Sorry, Ljuba, this is my daughter, Jennifer—

JENNY Please don't call me that. I'm not a puppy.

LORRAINE Okay, sorry, you're not. (*to Ljuba*) She goes by "Darby" now because, "why not?"

Ljuba is almost hyperventilating.

LJUBA Oh my goodness, oh my goodness! I thought I am going to die.

JENNY I go by Darby because you gave me a shit name that's stuck in your antiquated binary bubble.

LORRAINE Well, I don't know anything about all that but you're right, Jennifer is a dumb name. We were running out of time at the hospital and couldn't agree on anything.

Lorraine enters the kitchen and heads toward the open sliding glass door. She kneels and tries to close it but it's stuck open.

God, it's freezing in here. Why the hell is the door open and what are you doing here so late?

JENNY I was just in the area.

LORRAINE Oh please, you haven't called us in months—

JENNY I've been busy.

LORRAINE Right. Why are you here?

Jenny considers telling her—but turns the tables on Ljuba:

JENNY Who are you?

LJUBA I'm Ljuba. I take care of you grandmother.

JENNY Ah, that makes sense. The sacrificial lamb. And how long have you been . . . filling in?

LJUBA I work here for maybe the last six months.

JENNY (*to Lorraine*) Not surprised. I should have known you were too selfish to take care of your own mother.

48

LJUBA   Oh, no no, Lorraine is not selfish, it's very difficult to—

LORRAINE   Ljuba is a professional, okay? She is trained to deal with people like your grandmother.

JENNY   And I'm sure you spend your days in that room with her, making her last days comforting and memorable.

LORRAINE   Actually, if you must know, I do not go in there because I don't want to get her sick.

JENNY   Right, sure—

LORRAINE   Excuse me. Your grandmother has a weakened immune system and I am surrounded by people from all walks of life because I'm working at the JCC, which hires mentally disturbed people to clean the bathrooms.

JENNY   Wow, mom. You really are a bastion of respect and equity. It was nice to meet you Ljuba, good luck with everything and, you know, I'm sorry that we middle-class Americans exist. Hopefully, we're an aberration in the grand scheme of things. See ya, Mom.

Jenny goes to the fridge and pulls out some bottles of water for the road—

LORRAINE   Can I at least drive you back home? I haven't heard from you in months.

JENNY   I'm sure you're heartbroken.

LORRAINE   You're my daughter.

JENNY   Aw, thanks. Take care Ljuba.

LORRAINE   Jenny—!

Jenny is at the open glass door, when:

LJUBA   Darby.

Jenny stops.

LJUBA Darby, please don't leave. (*beat*) Maybe you stay five minutes. See your mother.

Jenny reenters and cracks open her bottle of water.

JENNY Where you from, Ljuba?

LJUBA Serbia. Is the former Yugoslavia.

JENNY Belgrade?

LJUBA No, Novi Sad area. Vojvodina. You know it?

JENNY Heard of it. Were you there in '99?

LJUBA What?

JENNY 1999?

LJUBA Yes, of course I was there—

JENNY Well then, my apologies on behalf of a pigheaded, jingoistic foreign policy.

LJUBA What do you mean?

JENNY I'm sorry we bombed you.

LJUBA Oh. Okay. Thank you.

JENNY 'Course.

LORRAINE She's my smart girl.

LJUBA I know. Harvard is a very good school! Congratulations!

JENNY What? I didn't go to Harvard.

LJUBA Oh.

LORRAINE I said it was *basically* Harvard. Don't sell yourself so short, honey. Emerson is right around the corner.

LJUBA She's just proud of you. She's your mother. Is normal, is nice.

JENNY Do you read Chomsky?

LJUBA   Um, is he Serbian?

JENNY (*laughing*)   No, no. But he opposed the bombing of your country. Really vocal about it. You should read *The New Military Humanism*.

LJUBA   What is this?

JENNY   It's a collection of essays about the hubris of American intervention around the world. How any time Americans get involved with something, they turn it to shit for their own selfish needs.

LJUBA (*at a loss*)   It sounds like a nice book. You read it?

JENNY   Years ago. You can probably get it online. Want me to write it down for you?

LJUBA   Um ... I can write it. You talk to your mother.

Ljuba heads to a little pad and begins to write down the name of the book she'll never read.

LJUBA   What is the name again?

JENNY   *The New Military Humanism.*

LJUBA   Right, yes, thank you.

LORRAINE   Okay—I'm sorry, can I please ask: What are you doing here?

Jenny pauses, stares her mother down.

JENNY   I came to see my grandmother.

LORRAINE   It's midnight.

LJUBA (*writing*)   Sorry—"*The New* ..."

JENNY   "*Military Humanism.*"

LJUBA   Oh. Sorry, thank you.

51

JENNY Yeah, I didn't want to see you. I took the train and walked here.

LORRAINE How do you think that makes me feel?

JENNY I actually don't care how it makes you feel.

LJUBA (*making a big show of the piece of paper*) I got it! Thank you so much for this interesting title.

JENNY No problem. I think you'll like it.

LJUBA Yes me too. *The New Military Humanism.*

LORRAINE So you decided to break in?

JENNY That door was always broken.

LORRAINE Yes, but your father always fixed it.

JENNY Not always.

LORRAINE Not always.

JENNY How is dad?

LORRAINE Not good, dear.

LJUBA Oh, Lorraine, don't be so negative. Bill is doing good, Darby, he just has attacks sometimes.

LORRAINE The doctors can't figure it out. He says it feels like being stabbed by electric knives and he wants to tear his skin off and jump into a fire.

LJUBA Yes, but he has a good sense of humor about it. And your mother keeps everything lighthearted, she is such a good caretaker. So I think is not too much trouble for him.

LORRAINE It's actually very scary for all of us.

JENNY When do they say he'll die?

LORRAINE Oh, sweetheart, MS is not a death sentence.

LJUBA   Yes, is maybe not comfortable for Bill but you don't have to worry about him dying.

Jenny smirks at Ljuba, onto her.

JENNY   You're very agreeable.

LJUBA (*confused*)   Thank you.

JENNY   What's my mother paying you?

LJUBA   Excuse me?

LORRAINE   Jennifer!

JENNY   What is she paying you to be so nice to her?

LJUBA   I take care of you *grandmother*.

JENNY   I know.

Ljuba looks to Lorraine, deeply uncomfortable.

JENNY   I'm moving to Manuel Antonio.

LORRAINE   Who's Manuel Antonio?

JENNY   It's a region in western Costa Rica. It's in the jungle.

LORRAINE   Oh, I didn't realize we just casually throw around names of regions in Costa Rica like we're all on board.

JENNY   I've discussed it before.

LORRAINE   Then I'll have to refer back to my diary.

LJUBA   It sounds beautiful.

JENNY   There she is! Right on time with the benign, manipulative compliment.

LJUBA   What do you mean?

JENNY   You really think it sounds beautiful?

LJUBA   The jungle? Of course. I grow up on a farm. The jungle is like a different planet.

JENNY (*realizing Ljuba was being sincere*)   Oh. Yeah, that makes sense. You grew up on a farm?

LJUBA   Yes, not anymore, but when I was a little girl, yes. We have pigs and cows and chicken.

JENNY   That's awesome. Were you guys totally self-sustainable?

LJUBA (*trying to give the right answer*)   Yes, I think maybe.

JENNY   That's cool. Zev and I are planning on raising chickens.

LORRAINE   Zev is her boyfriend—

JENNY   My husband.

LJUBA   Oh, congratulations.

LORRAINE   They're not married.

JENNY   Actually we got married in March.

LORRAINE   Oh.

JENNY   Yeah.

LORRAINE   I'm—congratulations to the both of you.

JENNY   Thanks.

> *Ljuba is uncomfortable with this tension—she goes to the pantry and takes out some chips and pours them into a large bowl. She gets some salsa from the fridge.*

LORRAINE   Am I allowed to ask when you're moving?

JENNY   Nobody thinks I should even be talking to you.

LORRAINE   You mentioned that the last time we spoke.

JENNY   They say you're toxic.

LORRAINE   You mentioned that too.

JENNY We're leaving next week.

LORRAINE And when are you coming back?

JENNY We're not.

LORRAINE Oh.

JENNY We worked it out with our papers—Americans can get residency if they invest over a certain amount and Zev's parents agreed to help us out—

LORRAINE How nice of them—

JENNY Yeah, it's pretty cool.

Lorraine looks like she might cry at the table. Ljuba sweeps in with chips and salsa.

LJUBA Hola! I have chips and salsa! For the Three Amigos!

JENNY Are you a real person?

LORRAINE She's dynamite.

LJUBA Oh stop it. It's just chips!

Ljuba sits down.

Lorraine looks at both women, with irony:

LORRAINE My two girls.

Pause.

LJUBA So you come to say goodbye to your grandmother before you leave. Is such a nice thing to do I think. Lorraine, isn't it a nice thing to do?

LORRAINE I actually didn't know that ... *Darby* liked her grandmother. They never really got along.

JENNY That's not true.

LORRAINE   Darling, I don't mean to contradict you but your nickname for her was "the shriveled cunt."

Ljuba coughs on a chip.

JENNY   That's because she looked like a shriveled cunt.

LORRAINE   Well, I'm sure there were other things that she looked like that had nicer names.

JENNY   Nope.

LORRAINE   And so you took the train out here in the middle of the night to avoid seeing me and your father, who is desperately sick, just so you can say goodbye to her?

JENNY   I wouldn't mind seeing Dad. Anyway, Zev and I have been accounting for our past actions and reevaluating our relationships and, when I was reevaluating Grandma, I realized that I had gotten her completely wrong and that I needed to apologize.

LORRAINE   Well, that's nice. Did you consider reevaluating me?

JENNY   Yeah, I did.
So I realized that I looked at Grandma as this fucking bitch, you know? She was nasty as hell. She treated people like shit. She never hugged me.

LORRAINE   But you decided to trek out to New Jersey to say goodbye to her?

JENNY   Yeah, because I realized—with the world she grew up in? How can you be anything else but a fucking bitch? Your fucking husband leaves you while you're pregnant?

LORRAINE   She was pregnant with me.

JENNY   Exactly. And she's supposed to put on a fake smile and pretend like everything's normal? Be some obsequious little Emily Post concubine? Fuck no. She scowled at strangers, she didn't tip waiters, she spit on the street. The world was, like, desperate for her to roll over and play dead so it could cannibalize her for its own patriarchal bullshit. But she refused and good for her, you know? Like, literally, the only possible, *normal* reaction to her life was to become a hardened bitch.

LORRAINE   And did you consider what growing up with that must have been like for me?

LJUBA   Must have been hard.

LORRAINE   Thank you, Ljuba.

LJUBA   She spit on the street?

LORRAINE   I didn't know about that.

JENNY   And I realized that I wouldn't have been able to become the person that I am today if I didn't have her as a role model. If I didn't have a strong woman like her to teach me that I didn't have to put on a fucking miniskirt and little girl voice to get people to like me.

Suddenly, Ljuba, fighting a rage inside of her, stands up and walks to the other side of the kitchen. She pushes against the stove, trying to calm herself.

Lorraine fights a trembling lip.

LORRAINE   Well, I'm very happy to hear you say that. It sounds like you're really doing some nice self-reflection.

JENNY   Yeah, thanks. It feels pretty good. I used to be so scared of her. Remember how you used to buy me a toy every time we went to see her to kind of, like, *bribe me*, I guess?

LORRAINE   I do remember that.

JENNY   And she used to yell at you.

LORRAINE   Mmhmm.

JENNY   "Why do you buy that girl everything she wants? You think she's gonna love you that way?"

LORRAINE   Right.

JENNY   God, I was so scared of her. But it's like, I was being raised in this bullshit consumerist culture where toys equaled love and hedonism equaled a good life, you know? I was literally just telling Zev that I'd probably be some stuck-up, yuppie cunt sequestered in the suburbs if it weren't for her.

There is a tense beat, until Ljuba can't take it anymore. She's on the verge of tears—

LJUBA   Excuse me, Darby. Can I say something to you?

JENNY (*as though nothing's wrong*)   Sure.

LJUBA   Do you think is nice, what you say to your mother?

JENNY (*pretending to not understand her accent*)   Do I "think is nice"? What?

LJUBA (*trying to rephrase*)   Do you think what you say to your mother is very nice?

LORRAINE   Ljuba, please, you don't need to intervene.

JENNY   Honestly, Ljuba, I don't really care if I'm being 'nice' or not.

LJUBA   You don't care about this?

LORRAINE   Ljuba, please. We're just joking around.

JENNY   No we're not.

LORRAINE   Well we're rehashing old times. It can get a little painful.

JENNY   I'm not in pain.

LORRAINE   And that's good. That's wonderful, sweetheart, I wouldn't want you to be in pain.

LJUBA   You want your mother to be hurt?

JENNY   I can't control how she feels.

LJUBA   But everything you say to her is like trying to kill her.

LORRAINE   Kill me!? Oh, Ljuba, let's not be overdramatic!

LJUBA   Is true, though. I listen. She finds every way she can to make you feel bad.

JENNY   You're very observant.

LJUBA (*emboldened*)   I don't know what that means!

JENNY   Then fuckin' stay out of it.

LORRAINE   Yes, Ljuba, please relax. Jennifer, let's speak more politely to Ljuba. English is her second language. And Ljuba, really, I'm fine—I think I know how to speak to my own daughter.

JENNY   Really? Do you?

LORRAINE   Well I would hope so. And Ljuba is just being overdramatic. Probably because of my influence! Let's leave the theatrics to the actress, shall we Ljuba?

JENNY   Yes, Ljuba! Let's leave the theatrics to my mother—the brilliant, groundbreaking artist! Starring three weekends in a row in *Fiddler on the Roof* or *Show Boat* or whatever the fuck dumbass, Zionist, Chitlin' Circuit, whitewashed bullshit playing at the local Jewish Community Center basement!

LORRAINE   Oh please honey—

JENNY   That I have to sit through my entire fucking life, applauding while my mother flaunts her asshole on stage in front of everyone I know, desperate for attention because she can't stand herself. Desperate for constant validation because she hates herself!

LORRAINE   I absolutely do not hate myself.

JENNY   Of course you hate yourself, you're just too distracted to realize it!

LORRAINE   Jenny!

JENNY   Desperate for strangers to love her, to think she's brilliant and hysterical because if she's left alone for one second, if she's not being *fawned over* for one second, she'll die! If she's not constantly applauded by the world, she'll suffocate!

LORRAINE   Jennifer, please—

JENNY   Yup, buy your tickets now before they run out of folding chairs!

LORRAINE   Jennifer!

JENNY   It's not "Jennifer," you bitch!

Suddenly, Ljuba slaps Jenny.

LJUBA   YOU RESPECT YOUR MOTHER!

BILL   What's going on?

The three women turn to the stairs to see Bill. Jenny behaves differently with Bill, sweet and childlike.

JENNY   Hi Daddy.

LJUBA   Excuse me, I go check on Ruthie.

Ljuba quickly darts into the bedroom.

LORRAINE   Bill! Sweetie! Did we wake you up? We were just having a little chat! I thought you were totally conked out sweetheart, I'm sorry. Look who's here!

Bill comes down the stairs, squinting in the dark.

BILL   Jennifer?

JENNY   Yeah.

BILL   What are you doing here?

JENNY   I just came to say goodbye.

LORRAINE   Isn't that sweet. Jennifer's taking a little vacation and she came to say goodbye to us. Isn't that nice?

BILL   Where are you going?

JENNY I'm just going to Costa Rica. With Zev. You liked Zev, remember?

BILL It's the middle of the night.

LORRAINE Yeah, isn't that funny! Always such a night owl!

BILL Can you give me a hug?

JENNY Yeah—

Jenny hugs Bill, choking up when she feels his back.

JENNY You're thin.

BILL No, I was always fat.

JENNY You're really thin, Daddy.

LORRAINE I think he looks fabulous. Everyone says he looks ten years younger! Can you believe that, sweetheart?

BILL No one says that.

LORRAINE Marjorie at the bank said that, Bill! You know that! I told you that! Marjorie, who works at the bank, said, "Bill looks ten years younger!"

There is a weird pause because everyone knows it's not true. Jenny is overcome, seeing her father in this state.

JENNY Do you feel very uncomfortable?

BILL Yes.

LORRAINE Well, he has good days and bad days, isn't that right Bill? Good days and bad days?

BILL I feel very uncomfortable.

JENNY I'm sorry.

LORRAINE Well let's not be such a downer, sweetie!

JENNY He's my father.

LORRAINE   I know that. I was there. But we try to keep things upbeat around here. Stress causes Bill to have some . . . not great moments.

JENNY   I can talk to my father the way I want. (*to Bill*) Is there anything you'd like to do?

BILL   Like what?

JENNY   I don't know. To change your situation. To be able to live out the life that you want. With the time you have left.

LORRAINE   My goodness, "the time he has left?" How are you talking to him?

JENNY   Because Zev and I are actually *moving* to Costa Rica.

BILL   You're moving?

JENNY   Yeah—it's really warm and comfortable and Zev's building a log cabin on this amazing mountain.

LORRAINE   You're living in a cabin?

JENNY   We're growing everything ourselves—it's all organic, fresh food. It's like a paradise. A thousand miles above sea level.

BILL   When are you moving there?

JENNY   Next week. But we could totally wait if you think you might be interested in coming—

LORRAINE   Oh, yes! Perfect! Take him to South America—

JENNY   —Central America—

LORRAINE   Excuse me! Take him to *Central America* with you so he can live in a little log cabin that your friend is building.

JENNY   My husband.

BILL   You got married?

LORRAINE   Surprise!

BILL You knew about this?

LORRAINE She just told me!

JENNY I would have told you, Daddy. I'm sorry.

BILL And you're moving away?

JENNY You can come with us!

LORRAINE That's a wonderful idea. And I assume you could also take the ten doctors we see every month and the world-class hospital which is only twenty minutes' drive away.

JENNY You should probably ask yourselves *why* you have to see so many doctors in a world-class hospital in the first place.

LORRAINE Because your father has a disease.

JENNY From what?

LORRAINE No one knows.

JENNY Well I'm sure it's really helpful being surrounded by the electrical grid and eating foods from the microwave.

BILL When did you get married?

JENNY March 18th.

BILL Why didn't you tell us?

JENNY I wanted to.

Bill begins rubbing on his leg, trying to fight off an attack.

LORRAINE Bill, calm down.

BILL You should have told us, Jennifer.

JENNY I'm sorry, Daddy.

BILL You should have told us.

LORRAINE Bill, you need to calm down. Take a breath.

BILL I'm going back to sleep.

JENNY   I love you, Daddy.

Bill shakes his head as he walks up the stairs. As he reaches the landing, he begins to have an attack.

This attack is worse than the previous one. He is writhing on the stairs.

LORRAINE   Jesus Christ!

JENNY   Holy shit, Daddy!

Jenny runs to her father. Lorraine is panicked.

LORRAINE   Ljuba!

JENNY   Mom! Do something!

LORRAINE   Ljuba!

JENNY   Mom, fucking do something!

LORRAINE   There's nothing to do!

JENNY   Call an ambulance!

LORRAINE   They can't do anything. This just happens. Ljuba!

Ljuba bursts out of the bedroom, having changed into her pajamas. She runs to Bill and places her hands on his shoulders.

LJUBA   It's okay, Mr. Bill, it's okay.

JENNY   What's happening to him?!

LJUBA   It's okay, Mr. Bill. You're okay.

As Bill calms:

It's okay. I take him upstairs.

LORRAINE   Thank you, Ljuba. Thank you, dear. (*to Bill*) I love you, sweetheart. You get some good rest. I love you so much, my sweet dear Bill.

JENNY   I love you Daddy.

Jenny and Lorraine watch as Ljuba helps Bill up. They are left alone.

JENNY   So you just stand there?

LORRAINE   What?

JENNY   You literally just stand there and do nothing? What a shitty fucking wife.

Beat. Then, Lorraine breaks—

LORRAINE   Get the fuck out of this house!

JENNY   Whoa!

LORRAINE   Get the fuck out of this house right now!

Lorraine picks up Jenny's messenger bag and throws it at her.

You will get the fuck out of here and you will never come back! You selfish little shitbag, you dirty little shitbag! You will get the fuck out of here and never come back. Do you hear me?!

JENNY   Mom!

LORRAINE   Go! Go! You go!

Lorraine is physically shoving Jenny out the door.

Lorraine reenters the house and walks around the empty kitchen, absorbing the horrible night. Wind blows in through the open sliding glass doors. She shivers. She tries to close the back door but, still, it will not budge.

Lorraine heads towards her mother's bedroom, inexplicably drawn to it. Ljuba appears on the stairs:

LJUBA   Lorraine.

LORRAINE   Yes, yes. I was just making sure she was all right.

Lorraine heads to the kitchen and busies herself.

LJUBA   She is all right. She is sleeping now.

LORRAINE   That's good, that's very good. She needs her rest.

LJUBA   You let me take care of her.

LORRAINE   Oh, of course. You're very capable, sweetheart.

LJUBA   Thank you, Ms. Lorraine.

LORRAINE   Why don't you go back upstairs and be with Bill? I'll clean up, dear.

LJUBA   I can clean. You are tired.

LORRAINE   I feel fine. I love cleaning. I love the routine, dear. I've always loved a routine.

LJUBA   Ms. Lorraine. You look at me.

LORRAINE   Yes?

LJUBA   You look at Ljuba now.

LORRAINE   Yes, dear?

LJUBA   You can stop smiling.

LORRAINE   What?

LJUBA   I know you. You can stop always smiling with me.

LORRAINE   I can?

LJUBA   Yes. You stop always smiling with me. And I stop always smiling with you. Okay?

LORRAINE   Okay.

LJUBA   Good.

Ljuba heads upstairs.

Lorraine tries to clean a bowl but it drops into the sink. She stifles tears, distraught—

She wanders around the house, flicking off each light.

The only light that remains is coming from her mother's bedroom.

Lorraine heads toward it, entering her mother's room for the first time—

SCENE 3

It is a week later, about 5pm.

The house has been cleaned except now, the broken sliding glass doors have been boarded over with plywood, shutting off the outside world.

Lorraine enters, coming down the stairs.

LORRAINE (*calling back upstairs to Bill*) I'll be right back up with your dinner, sweetheart. Don't suddenly nod off, okay? You have the absolute worst timing!

Lorraine takes a few Tupperware out of the refrigerator.

They should be back here any minute and I don't want to be stuck upstairs spoon-feeding a sleeping giant!

Lorraine begins plating the food.

Ronny is so gorgeous, isn't he? Taking Ljuba out so much. He really goes so far above and beyond, which is also reflected in his work in the show. What he lacks in stage presence and charisma he really makes up for in dedication. I just cherish our time on stage together.

I mean the whole cast—it's such an unbelievably supportive group of people. And everyone loves me. It really is like a family for me, a real family.

Lorraine puts the plate in the microwave. While it heats, she fills a glass with ice water.

You know, it's funny—I didn't even realize that the whole cast has been going out for drinks after Friday and Saturday rehearsals. Even James Peter! Can you believe it? No one ever told me! Ronny told

Ljuba, who let it slip! Loose lips on that girl! Beautiful, but loose, right?

Isn't that just so sweet of them to not tell me? They know how seriously I take the show and that I'd be absolutely horrified if I knew they were all going out and getting fuddled at some cheap dive! The last thing we need is for them all to die in a drunk driving accident the week before opening!

She now prepares a serving tray with utensils and napkins.

And just picturing James Peter soused is enough to keep me indoors! (*doing an impression of a drunk James Peter*) Letsh take it from the top! (*sings, drunkenly*) "Shom enchanted evening! You may drink too many! You may feel hungover! And show up late to work!" (*laughing at herself*) Can you imagine it? Ah, James Peter. (*acts like a drunk James Peter giving notes*) Lorraine! Stop doing so much! You do too much on stage! (*as herself*) Oh sorry, James Peter! Sorry for making an effort and fully investing in my character! (*as a drunk James Peter*) The scene is not about you! You're too loud. You're too loud. (*as herself, misquoting Churchill*) I may be too loud, but in the morning I will be quiet! And you will still be James Peter!

She cackles to herself. Then, more seriously:

Too scared to actually step on that stage! Hiding in your little director's chair! It takes true courage to get off that perch and expose yourself. To climb down from your high horse and step on those boards every night. True courage. Do you have it, James? That's the question. (*then, suddenly lighthearted*) I'll probably join them at the bar one night. I know they would all just *flip* if I showed up. Without warning. I'd just saunter in like I'd been there all along. "Hi Chuck! Hi Tommy! Hi Kelly DiSanto! Surprised to see me?" Stuffy Lorraine, always in character, finally lets loose and has a few beers. I can party with the rest of them! I can drink you under the table, Kelly DiSanto!

The microwave dings. Lorraine takes the hot plate out of the microwave and places it on the tray.

68

Okay, I have beef stew and mashed potatoes. A real man's meal! Like you're building a bridge or fighting in Normandy! Your calloused hands, pawing at the grub—

She begins heading up the stairs with the tray of food and water.

I just love the way you're eating these days. Your appetite knows no bounds!

Lorraine disappears upstairs. The house is quiet.

After a moment, the front door opens and Ljuba and Ronny enter, laughing and holding two boxes of chocolates. Ronny is doing a funny French accent.

RONNY   Normally is twenty-five dollars, but for you, Madame, is *free*!

Ljuba cracks up laughing as they take off their jackets. Ljuba tries the French accent:

LJUBA   For you, Madame, is *free*.

RONNY   How is that not totally sleazy?

LJUBA   If someone wants to give me something for free, is not sleazy! I am now accepting a sleazy car and a sleazy house! I don't care! This is my new rule!

RONNY   Ah, very convenient rule!

LJUBA (*calls up the stairs*)   Lorraine! We're back!

LORRAINE (*os*)   Be down in a second, sweetheart. Is Ronny here too?

RONNY (*in the French accent*)   I am here. *Madame.*

Ljuba bursts out laughing as she peeks into the bedroom to check on Ruthie and drop off her purse.

And we come bearing chocolates!

LJUBA   Yes, French chocolates!

RONNY   Don't worry—we have a box for you too.

LJUBA   And that box, Madame, was *free!*

Ronny and Ljuba laugh as Lorraine appears from the stairs.

LORRAINE   Hello, Lootellans!

RONNY (*sings*)   "Bloody Mary's walking down the stairs!"

LJUBA   So, how was Ruthie? Did she ring me?

LORRAINE   Nope, nothing. Not a peep. I think she's been napping the whole time.

LJUBA   She still is, I just check on her.

LORRAINE   That woman would sleep through a war.

LJUBA   Thank you so much for watching her.

LORRAINE   Are you kidding? She's my mother! And I just love the idea of you two going on romantic dates so I can live vicariously through you. I don't care that it's all fake. In fact, I prefer it. It adds to the fantasy! So where did you go? What did you do? I want details!

RONNY   Well, if it's romance you're looking for, you'll be pleased to know that we decided to have a picnic in that park right off Route Nine.

LJUBA (*in on the deadpan humor*)   Yes, maybe you know it because it's right near the biggest cemetery I ever see in my whole life.

LORRAINE   Oh, god. I know exactly where you're talking about. Very charming, Ronny.

RONNY   Oh, come on, the park part was nice. If you kind of don't face the cemetery!

LJUBA   It was hard to miss.

LORRAINE   Did you at least get some good pictures?

RONNY   We did! I bought a bottle of French wine and chocolates and we stood over this little pond—the part that wasn't totally covered in bird poop!—and took some lovely shots.

LJUBA   Yes, Ronny kept saying that it looks like the south part of France, right?

RONNY   I swear, it looked like we were picnicking in Saint-Tropez. Of course I've never actually been to Saint-Tropez, but I always imagined it looks like a tiny suburban park near a cemetery!

LORRAINE   Ooh! Enchanté!

RONNY   Okay, I hate to be a party pooper, but I should probably get back home. Steven's cooking tonight and if I'm late he'll think I'm trying to avoid eating his food—because I always am!

LJUBA   You are too much!

RONNY   I told him I'd just drop you off, grab the money, and head back home.

LORRAINE   Oh, Steven is such a wet blanket! Stay!

LJUBA   Yes, stay!

RONNY   Sorry, like Harry the Horse, I'm here to collect 'da money for 'da marriage!

LJUBA   Okay, I will go get your sack of money, Mr. Horse! Be right back—

Ljuba heads to the bedroom but stops before she enters—

I enter this room a poor servant, but I shall return a rich queen.

LORRAINE   Honey, you were born a queen.

Ljuba exits into the bedroom.

RONNY   Well, that makes two of us.

LORRAINE   You are too much! Sit down, you're rocking the boat. She just gets better and better, doesn't she?

RONNY   She's a saint. Oh wait! Did I tell you what I was thinking of doing tomorrow—*if* James Peter doesn't completely hate me for it?

LORRAINE   I think he already might, but what?

RONNY   Okay, tell me if this is way too much, but what if my character has a limp?

Ljuba enters from the bedroom. She is in a strange state.

LORRAINE   A limp? Jesus, Ronny, can you be any more hammy?

RONNY   How is that hammy? People have limps. It's a real thing!

Ljuba approaches Lorraine, coming oddly close to her face.

LORRAINE   One second dear.

Ljuba ambles back into the bedroom, in a daze.

You're already a stretch as the virile Marine, let's not make the audience work too hard.

RONNY   But think about it! I've been fighting in the war, everyone else has just been lounging around on the island. Maybe I should have something to show for it!

Suddenly, the bedroom door swings open and Ljuba races out, charging at Lorraine!

LJUBA   Where is it?! Where is it Lorraine?!

LORRAINE   Where is what, dear?

LJUBA   Where is it!

Ljuba shakes Lorraine, who easily unlatches herself. Lorraine remains eerily calm.

LORRAINE   Ljuba, honey, you're going to have to calm down and—

LJUBA   WHAT DID YOU DO WITH MY MONEY!?

LORRAINE   The money for Ronny?

In Ljuba's panic, her English grammar suffers.

LJUBA   YES MONEY FOR RONNY!

LORRAINE   It's missing?

LJUBA   YOU KNOW IS MISSING!

LORRAINE   How would I know it's missing?

LJUBA   I count it two hour ago! I see it with my own eye two hour ago! I count it right before I leave the house! TWO HOUR AGO!

LORRAINE   Well a lot can happen in two hours, sweetheart.

RONNY   Lorraine, what's going on?

LORRAINE   I have no idea—she's clearly upset.

RONNY   Ljuba, did you check carefully?

LJUBA   Of course I check carefully. Is my whole life. My daughter life! (*to Lorraine*) Please say you are make a joke, Lorraine. Please say you are make a joke.

LORRAINE   Ah, you know what probably happened? Jenny probably broke in here again and took it. That little scamp.

LJUBA   Jenny not take it!

LORRAINE   Are you sure? She's very crafty, very wily.

LJUBA   Only you know where it is!

LORRAINE   I'd love to help you, Ljuba, but accusing me is not a good way to start.

Ljuba begins frantically scouring the house, overturning couch cushions, ripping things out of kitchen cabinets.

RONNY   Lorraine, what did you do?

LORRAINE   I didn't do anything! I've just been home, alone, cooking lunch and taking care of my mother so that you and Ljuba can have a nice day out in the park.

Ljuba shrieks and flies in Lorraine's face—

LJUBA   *You* tell me to go out! You tell me, "Oh the sun is shining and is such a beautiful day, why not you and Ronny go out for a nice date?"

LORRAINE   Oh, so now it's my fault that the sun is shining? What else did I do?

LJUBA (*full of pent-up rage*)   *You know everything wrong that you do.*

LORRAINE   Well what is that supposed to mean?

Ronny tries to intervene but Ljuba shoves him out of the way.

Ljuba, honey, I'm sure that Ronny would marry you without the money. I bet Steven would love having all three of you around the house.

Ronny is deeply uncomfortable. Ljuba glances back at Ronny—

RONNY   I—I—Lorraine how could you—

LJUBA   AHH!

RONNY   Ljuba!!

Ljuba screams in Lorraine's face and then darts upstairs to look for the money.

Ronny and Lorraine are alone.

We hear a racket from upstairs.

Lorraine, are you okay?

LORRAINE   I'm great, why?

RONNY   Ljuba told me about Bill.

LORRAINE   Told you what?

RONNY That he's in the hospital.

LORRAINE Bill's not in the hospital, dear. He's right upstairs. (*calls upstairs*) Be up in a minute, sweetie! Ronny sends his regards.

RONNY Ljuba said he's been in the hospital for the last few days.

LORRAINE I think I would know if my own husband was in the hospital, please dear.

RONNY Lorraine—

LORRAINE Now, Ronny, honey, would you be a dear and head home?

RONNY Did you take Ljuba's money?

LORRAINE Of course I didn't do anything of the sort. I don't know what she's talking about. That money is for *you*—for the *two of you* to start your wonderful new life together.

RONNY Lorraine, you're scaring me.

LORRAINE Oh, sweetheart, I'm sorry. I don't mean to scare you. But I think it's best if you head home to Steven—despite his terrible cooking! And I'll see you at rehearsal tomorrow.

RONNY I don't think I should leave.

LORRAINE I think you should.

Lorraine begins moving Ronny toward the door. Ronny tries to call up to Ljuba:

RONNY Ljuba!

LORRAINE You really do have to leave now, Ronny. Thank you again for taking her out. She really has so few good people in her life.

RONNY Ljuba, I am so sorry! I'll call you.

Lorraine opens the door and forces Ronny out—

LORRAINE Work on your limp! You know, now that I think about it, I actually think it'll be great. James Peter is sure to love it!

RONNY (*calling back in to Ljuba*) I'm so sorry, Ljuba, I'm so sorry.

LORRAINE Get home safely, Ronny.

She shuts the door on him and locks it. After a moment, Ljuba reenters from the stairs, haggard and in a state of shock.

Hi sweetheart, did you find what you were looking for?

Ljuba ambles toward Lorraine, not sure whether she wants to punch her or collapse into her arms.

We can call the police to report it missing, but I'm just so worried they'll find out you're here illegally and take you away.

Lorraine bear hugs Ljuba and steers her toward a chair.

Good girl, come here and sit down.

Ljuba slumps into the chair. She is rocking back and forth, distraught, occasionally mumbling:

LJUBA What I do? What I do?

LORRAINE Now, Ljuba, sweetie, I understand you're upset. I'd probably be upset if I were in your position too. But luckily, I'm in my position, so I can more clearly see what you're going through.

LJUBA What I do? What I do?

LORRAINE When you're on the inside of something, it's almost impossible to see things clearly. It's actually one of the beautiful things about inhabiting a role and fully committing, which of course, has always been my specialty.

LJUBA (*to herself*) I have to call my daughter.

LORRAINE She's not awake now, honey. It's too late.

LJUBA Moram nazvati svoju kćer.

Lorraine moves to give her a massage but Ljuba aggressively shrugs Lorraine off.

You don't touch me!

LORRAINE   Ljuba, sweetheart, it's me. Listen, I understand you're upset about Ronny. He was a good catch but there are other men out there. We're gonna have to wash that man right outta—

Lorraine tries, again, to comfort Ljuba but Ljuba pushes her off and moves to sit on the floor, her head in her hands

These things happen. You couldn't have expected it to work out perfectly on the very first try. That's just hubris, dear. In a way, Ronny was too good to be true. Now. The *worst*-case scenario is you stay here with me, work for another few years and save up the money to try again. Unless you're totally bored of me! Which I can understand!

LJUBA   Lorraine!!!

LORRAINE   I'm very boring! Aren't I just a big old bore?

LJUBA   LORRAINE!!!

Lorraine moves to Ljuba and massages her shoulders. Unlike before, Ljuba is spent and just succumbs to it.

LORRAINE   Now, I don't know about you, but I think the two of us make a great team. And if we can't find the money, we'll just go on the run together—like Roxie Hart and Velma Kelly. I'd be Velma because I'm brassy and a natural alto. And you're totally Roxie, reckless and cute, with your whole life ahead of you! And of course, they were *both* incredibly beautiful—

We hear a beep from the other room.

Just like us.

There is another beep.

Pause.

Another beep.

Aren't you going to check on her?

Ljuba finally takes her head out of her hands and looks up at Lorraine, horrified by her.

Beep beep beep.

Ljuba turns and walks into the bedroom.

She'll be stuck here forever.

Lorraine turns, exhales, and, in good spirits, says to herself:

LORRAINE Well!

We hear the jaunty opening chords of "I'm Gonna Wash That Man Right Outta My Hair."

Lorraine begins moving brightly to the music as though she is hearing it as well.

As Mitzi Gaynor starts singing, we begin to fade out.

END